© Franklin Watts 1994

Franklin Watts
95 Madison Avenue
New York, NY 10016

10 9 8 7 6 5 4 3 2 1

Library of Congress Cataloging-in-Publication Data

Baxter, Nicola.
Invaders and Settlers/Nicola Baxter
p. cm. -- (Craft Topics)
Includes bibliographical references and index
ISBN 0-531-14338-4
1. Great Britain--History--Invasions--Juvenile Literature.
2. Land settlement--Great Britain--History--Juvenile Literature.
3. Handicraft--Juvenile Literature. (1. Great Britain--History--
Invasions. 2. Land settlement--Great Britain. 3. Handicraft.)
I. Title. II. Series.
DA50. B3 1994
941--dc20   93-46464
                                   CIP AC

Editor: Hazel Poole
Designed by: Sally Boothroyd
Artwork by: Ed Dovey
Photography by: Peter Millard
Additional picture research by: Juliet Duff

CONTENTS

THE FAR EDGE OF EUROPE

From the earliest times, people have traveled from their homes to find better lives for themselves and their families. The new skills, ideas, and languages that they bring to the country where they settle may change forever the lives of the people already living there and the history of the country itself.

At the time when Celtic peoples were moving westward into Britain, the great civilizations of Greece and Rome grew up around the Mediterranean. From small beginnings in Rome, the Roman Empire spread in all directions. In the first century A.D., Britain became the most northerly part of the Roman Empire.

A THOUSAND YEARS OF INVASIONS

It is almost a thousand years since Britain was last invaded and conquered by an army from overseas. This was when the Normans, under the leadership of Duke William of Normandy, invaded in 1066. But for a thousand years before that, many different peoples came to settle in the British Isles. They knew that Britain had rich supplies of wood, metal, and farm produce. The changes that these invaders brought are still part of British life today.

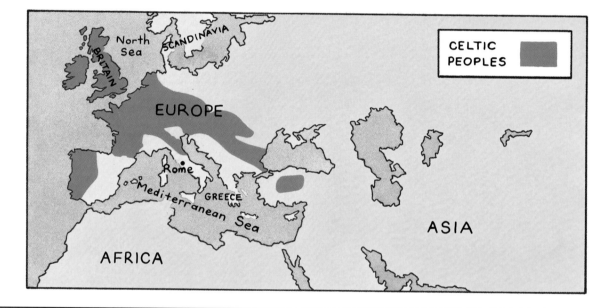

3500 B.C. onward people from western Europe settle in Britain.

55 B.C. The Roman Julius Caesar arrives in Britain.

A.D. 43 The Romans invade southern Britain.

A.D. 406 The Romans leave Britain. The Anglo-Saxons begin to invade northern and eastern Britain.

THE ANCIENT BRITONS

The people who lived in Britain 2,000 years ago are known as Britons, but they, too, had come from more eastern parts of Europe. They were of Celtic origin, the ancestors of many of the people who live in Wales today. The roots of their Celtic languages can still be traced in modern Welsh and Gaelic languages.

The time in which the ancient Britons lived is known as the Iron Age because they made and used iron tools. In fact, the Celts were very skilled at working many kinds of metal.

Most Celts lived by farming. Large family groups farmed the land and raised animals for food and clothing. Traces of their fields can sometimes be seen today, but more obvious are the huge mounds of earth that they built to protect themselves from attack.

▲ *Many Iron Age earthworks can still be seen. This fort at Maiden Castle in Dorset was protected by four great earth walls.*

We cannot read what the Celtic Britons themselves felt and thought because until the Roman invasion they did not read or write. Their knowledge of what had happened came from spoken stories or songs. This is called oral history.

The Celts in Britain were not isolated from the rest of Europe. Traders brought goods from other parts of the Roman Empire long before the Roman invasion.

793 The Vikings begin to raid Britain.

878 King Alfred defeats the Vikings.

1066 The Normans invade Britain.

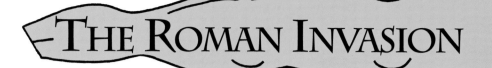

THE ROMAN INVASION

By the time the Romans invaded Britain in A.D. 43, they already had a vast empire. They were used to taking over new lands and people, and had very efficient armies and army commanders who knew how to take control quickly and completely.

At the time of the invasion, the Romans had already had contact with parts of Britain for nearly a hundred years. In 55 B.C. Julius Caesar, who had been fighting in what is now France, crossed the English Channel and subdued a few tribes. His visit may have been meant only as a warning to the Britons not to help the French tribes fight the Romans.

About 40,000 Roman soldiers took part in the invasion of A.D. 43. They had better weapons than the British troops and they were more carefully trained and organized. Some tribes fought hard against the invaders, but others were happy to welcome new opportunities to trade with the whole Roman Empire.

As soon as the southeast was secure, the Emperor Claudius himself came to accept the surrender of the local leaders of the British tribes at what is now Colchester in Essex.

This bronze shield shows the skill of Celtic craftsmen before the Roman invasion. They used beautifully flowing designs to decorate their metalwork. The shield was found in the River Thames. ▶

▲ *Before they could get close to the Romans, the British soldiers were attacked by a hail of javelins. In close fighting, their longer swords were difficult to use and, unlike the Romans, they had very little armor.*

MAKE A CELTIC SHIELD

Ask a grown-up to help you with this, since you will need to do some cutting.

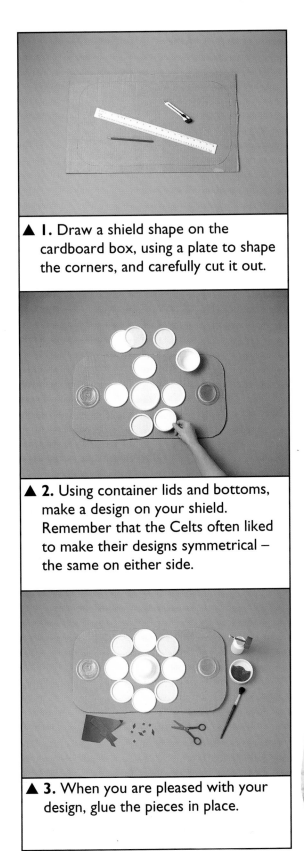

▲ **1.** Draw a shield shape on the cardboard box, using a plate to shape the corners, and carefully cut it out.

▲ **2.** Using container lids and bottoms, make a design on your shield. Remember that the Celts often liked to make their designs symmetrical – the same on either side.

▲ **3.** When you are pleased with your design, glue the pieces in place.

You will need: a large piece of thick cardboard ● a small plate ● a modeling knife ● empty plastic food containers and lids of various sizes ● a pencil ● a ruler ● acrylic glue ● bronze-colored paint ● sharp scissors ● colored paper or plastic "jewels"

4. Paint the whole shield a bronze color and add pieces of colored paper and plastic "jewels" as decoration.

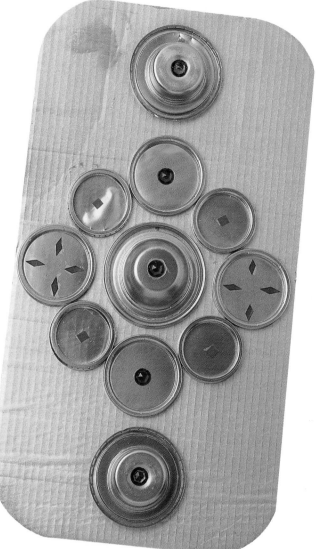

THE ROMANS IN BRITAIN

We know much more about the period when the Romans were in Britain than we do about earlier times. The Romans left written records of their activities, as well as many carved notices, called inscriptions, on monuments and buildings.

GOVERNING A NEW LAND

As a province of the Roman Empire, Britain had a Roman governor who was responsible for running the country. He appointed local governors for towns and areas. The Roman army was always active to remind people of the Romans' strength and to tackle any uprisings that took place. Many Roman soldiers settled in Britain when they retired.

Roman towns were built to a similar plan all over the empire, with straight streets, shops, and houses, and a central marketplace called the forum. The Romans imported goods and food from all over the empire, helping Roman settlers to feel at home. Food plants such as carrots and peas were also introduced by the Romans. ▼

Tribes in the north of Scotland were never conquered by the Romans. In the second century A.D., the Emperor Hadrian had a wall built to stop them from raiding farther south. It was 75 miles (120 kilometers) long.

NEW WAYS OF LIVING

The Roman invaders brought many new ideas with them. Before the Romans came, there were no towns in Britain, only small villages. London, now the biggest city in Britain, was founded by the Romans.

A WRITTEN LANGUAGE

The language of the Romans was Latin. They used it throughout their empire and every Roman soldier had to be able to read and write. Of course, Britons who lived and traded with the Romans had to learn Latin and many of them in the towns could read and write as well. For hundreds of years after the Romans left Britain, Latin was still used for official documents and in the Christian religion.

▲The Romans were skilled engineers. Their houses had plumbing and heating and they built roads and bridges throughout Britain. The Britons must have been astonished by the speed at which people and goods could be moved about the province.

This Roman mosaic floor from Fishbourne shows Cupid riding a dolphin, surrounded by sea beasts, sea horses, and sea panthers.

MANY BELIEFS

During the time that the Romans were in Britain, the new religion of Christianity, based on the teachings of Jesus Christ, began to spread to all parts of the empire.

The religion of the ancient Britons was closely linked to the natural world and the importance of the seasons and the fertility of the soil. Priests called druids led ceremonies and made predictions. The religion of the Romans featured many gods, some of whom also represented the rhythms of nature.

As long as local religions did not threaten their rule, the Romans let them continue. At first the Romans tried to stop Christianity because Christians claimed that their first duty was to God, not to earthly rulers, but later even the Roman emperors became Christians.

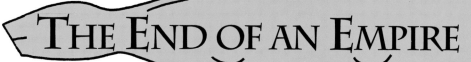

For nearly 400 years the Romans ruled a large part of the British Isles. Sometimes the Britons lived peacefully under Roman rule. But very often the Romans had to cope with uprisings by some of the British tribes or attacks from outside the borders of the empire.

A famous revolt happened only 16 years after the invasion. It was led by Boudica, queen of the Iceni tribe from East Anglia. Boudica's troops burned down the town of Colchester and went on to attack and destroy London. The Roman governor, Suetonius, hurried back from Anglesey, where he was attacking other tribes, and crushed the British revolt.

A later Roman historian described Boudica as having red hair and "a large golden necklace." It may have been like this neck ring, called a torque, found in Norfolk.

The problems that the Romans had in keeping order in Britain happened throughout the empire. As the empire grew, there were more people to control and more tribes outside the empire wanting to attack and steal from wealthy citizens. In A.D. 406, the Roman army finally left Britain to defend other parts of the empire. The end of the empire was very near and the Romans never returned.

The Roman army was divided into legions and every legion had a standard called an "eagle." It was used as a rallying point during battles and was fiercely guarded.

MAKE A ROMAN STANDARD AND WREATH

You will need: a rounded stick or garden stake at least 3 feet (1 meter) long ● cardboard ● a pencil ● a potted plant stake ● a paper plate ● paper ● a piece of red or purple cloth ● scissors ● transparent tape or glue ● gold paint

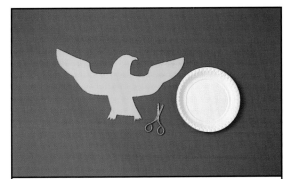

▲ **1.** Draw an eagle shape as shown on a piece of cardboard and cut it out carefully. It should be about twice as wide as the paper plate.

2. On another piece of cardboard, place the paper plate and draw around part of it to make a crescent shape. Then cut it out.

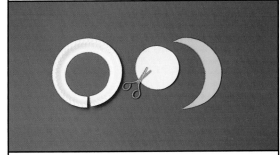

▲ **3.** Carefully cut out the flat middle part of the paper plate, making sure to cut the plate rim in only one place.

▲ **4.** Paint all the cut-out pieces and the potted plant stake gold. Paint a piece of paper gold on both sides and cut out lots of leaf shapes. Use tape to attach the leaves to the paper plate rim to make a wreath.

▲ **5.** Hang the red or purple cloth from the potted plant stake. You can fray the bottom edge of the cloth and paint it to make a gold fringe. Use tape to attach the eagle, crescent, and potted plant stake to the stick or garden stake.

11

A NEW THREAT

While the Romans were in Britain, they defended their province from attacks by overseas tribes. But when the Roman army had gone, the British were at the mercy of invaders from northern Europe. Almost immediately, the people known as Anglo-Saxons began to attack the northeast coast of England.

WHO WERE THE ANGLO-SAXONS?

The people that we call Anglo-Saxons actually came from several different tribes: the Jutes from what is now Denmark, the Angles from northern Germany, and the Saxons and Frisians from parts of Germany and the Netherlands. Their pirate ships had raided the coast of Britain for years, but when the Romans left they were able to push farther into the country with greater numbers of people.

The parts of Europe where the Anglo-Saxons lived were difficult to farm. They were wooded and marshy, with some areas being flooded by the sea. There was not enough good land to feed everyone, so the Anglo-Saxons hoped to find better farming land in Britain.

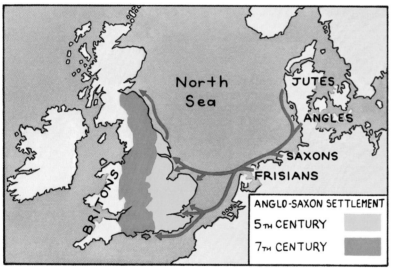

North Sea

JUTES

ANGLES

SAXONS

FRISIANS

BRITONS

ANGLO-SAXON SETTLEMENT

5TH CENTURY

7TH CENTURY

▲ As the Anglo-Saxons gradually occupied more and more of Britain, they pushed some of the Celtic Britons farther westward. But other Britons lived peacefully alongside the newcomers. It is from the Angles that we get the words "England" and "English."

The Anglo-Saxons crossed the North Sea in big wooden rowing boats like this. The large oar was the rudder, used to steer the boat. The rowers pulled their oars against the slots on the side of the boat. This boat was found in a peat bog in Denmark. ▼

THE ANGLO-SAXON STORY OF THE INVASION

Over 400 years after the Anglo-Saxons began to arrive, King Alfred ordered that a book should be written to tell the history of the Anglo-Saxons in Britain. This book has survived and is called The Anglo-Saxon Chronicle. The book says that after the Romans left, a British king called Vortigern gave some Saxons land in southeast England in return for helping him to fight the Picts, a Scottish tribe that the Romans never conquered. Angles and Jutes, as well as Saxons, came to Britain, led by two brothers, Hengist and Horsa. After they had helped the king, the Chronicle says, they turned against him and took over the kingdom.

▲ This is a page from the Anglo-Saxon Chronicle. As the story was written down a long time after the events it describes, it is hard to tell whether it is true, but it is certainly possible that some Anglo-Saxons were invited to Britain.

How Anglo-Saxons Lived

The Anglo-Saxons did not invade Britain all at once but gradually moved down the rivers and settled farther and farther west and south. In some places Roman systems of government may have continued for up to 200 years after the Romans left. Meanwhile, some Celtic British groups were returning to the way of life they followed before the Romans came. So for some time there was a great mixture of people and ways of life in Britain.

The Anglo-Saxon farmers grew peas, beans, barley, and wheat as well as hay for their animals to eat in the winter. They kept cattle, sheep, pigs, geese, and hens. They also seem to have had pet cats and dogs.

Many pieces of Anglo-Saxon pottery have been found. Most of these were for everyday use, but some pots were used as urns in which to bury the ashes of dead people.

There was no tea or coffee in England in Anglo-Saxon times. Poor people drank a kind of beer, while rich people had wine or mead, a drink made from honey and water.

Most Anglo-Saxon clothes were made from wool. They raised the sheep, spun, dyed, and wove the wool themselves. The weaving looms had stones with holes in them to weight down the threads. They were used leaning against the wall of a house.

Clothes were held together with brooches. Women wore strings of colored glass or stone beads. Some women wore strange keylike metal objects from their waists. Archaeologists are not sure what these were for. What do you think?

AN ANGLO-SAXON VILLAGE

Anglo-Saxon homes were usually built with a wooden framework. The walls were filled in with wooden planks or clay mixed with straw. Some of them seem to have had a space under the floor, perhaps for storage or to keep the floor dry.

A family home was quite small and probably had only one room. But the village also had a larger building, called a hall, where people could meet and eat together.

MAKE AN ANGLO-SAXON HALL

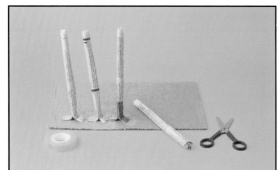

▲ **1.** Make a rectangular base about 14 inches (35 cm) long and 8 ¹/₄ inches (20 cm) wide from a piece of strong cardboard. Then fold pieces of newspaper in halves and quarters and roll them up tightly. Use glue or tape to make sure they don't unroll. Make two cuts at the end off each roll and glue or tape them evenly around the rectangle to make posts for your hall.

▲ At West Stow in Suffolk, archaeologists have discovered traces of an Anglo-Saxon village. After finding post holes in the ground, they were able to work out where the village buildings were, and to make some good guesses about how they were built. Then they used this knowledge to rebuild the village using the same tools and methods that the Anglo-Saxons used.

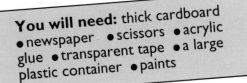

You will need: thick cardboard
● newspaper ● scissors ● acrylic glue ● transparent tape ● a large plastic container ● paints

2. Trim the posts so that they are all the same level but shape the end ones as shown. Tape or glue more paper rolls across the posts as in the picture to make the framework for the roof and doors and windows.

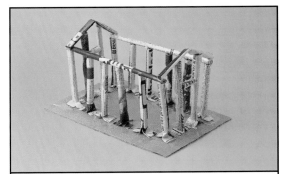

▲ **3.** Tear some more newspaper into small pieces and soak them overnight in water in the plastic container.

4. Mash up the paper a bit more with your fingers. Then squeeze out as much water as possible and mix in some acrylic glue. Add enough so that the paper can be modeled into different shapes.

5. Use the paper mixture to fill in the walls of the hall, just as the Anglo-Saxons used clay and straw. Remember to leave some spaces for windows and doors.

Why not make lots of Anglo-Saxon buildings of different sizes and build a model village?

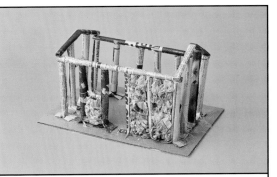

▲ **6.** When the paper mixture has dried, make a cardboard roof for your hall and put it carefully on top of the walls. Make sure it has a hole in the middle for smoke from the fire to come out.

▲ **7.** Paint your model and its base. You can add cardboard doors as well if you like.

RELIGIOUS LIFE

Christianity had come to Britain in Roman times, but the Anglo-Saxons brought their own religion. They believed that different gods controlled different parts of their lives and what would happen to them after they died.

Woden was the chief of all the gods. Frig, his wife, made crops grow. Tiu was the war god, and Thunor the god of thunder and the sky.

Our only clues to how the Anglo-Saxons worshiped their gods come from the writings of Christian missionaries who said that they killed animals in their religious ceremonies. But the missionaries were trying to stamp out the Anglo-Saxon religion, so it is hard to know if this is true.

This Anglo-Saxon helmet and buckle are beautifully decorated. Often, Anglo-Saxon decorations contained images of the god Woden.

These objects were found in a grave at Sutton Hoo in Suffolk. An important man had been buried in a wooden boat that was 92 feet (28 meters) long. Many precious objects were buried with him. Although this was not a Christian burial, some objects with biblical names were found in the grave. ▼

18

AN ANGLO-SAXON BURIAL

Many of the pieces of Anglo-Saxon jewelry, goods, and clothing that have been found were discovered in graves. In pagan (not Christian) burials, it seems that people were buried with some of their precious possessions, perhaps because it was thought that they would need them in the next life.

THE RETURN OF CHRISTIANITY

By the time the Anglo-Saxons had been in Britain for about 200 years, Christianity was still practiced in only a few western areas. Pope Gregory, the leader of the Christian religion in western Europe, sent a man called Augustine to England to convert the people to Christianity.

Christians believe that there is only one God and that he sent Jesus Christ to live on earth and show people how to act in this life and how they can live forever with God after they die.

Augustine's first success was in converting Aethelbert, an Anglo-Saxon king living in Kent. The king allowed Augustine to use an old Roman church in Canterbury. Pope Gregory made Augustine Archbishop of Canterbury. This has been the title of the leader of the main Christian church in Britain ever since.

MONASTERIES

Because the Anglo-Saxons did not invade Ireland, the people there were still Christians since Roman times. About 30 years before Augustine came to England, an Irish monk called Columba sailed to Iona, a small island off the western coast of Scotland, and built a monastery.

Monks are men who have decided to live together and make worshiping God the most important part of their lives. The place where they live is called a monastery. Women who do the same thing are called nuns. They live in a nunnery or convent.

Christianity spread across northern England, and another famous monastery was built on the island of Lindisfarne, just off the coast of Northumbria.

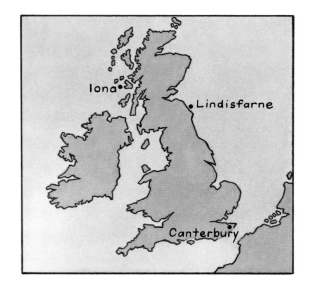

▲Lindisfarne's isolated position off the coast, later made it easy for raider's from the sea to attack.

Monasteries were important centers of learning for hundreds of years. The monks studied the Bible, the book that describes the life of Jesus Christ and the history of the people he lived among, and many other subjects. They wrote books by hand and often decorated them with beautiful colored drawings.

◀This is a page from the Lindisfarne Gospels. The Gospels are the part of the Bible that describes the life of Jesus. The book was copied out by hand and has many beautiful decorations. It is written in the Latin language on vellum, which is made from calf's skin.

MAKE AN ILLUMINATED MANUSCRIPT

You will need: thick white or cream paper • some strong, cold tea • a sponge • a pencil • felt-tip pens • a gold felt-tip pen

▲ **1.** Dip the sponge in the cold tea and dab it across the paper to make it look old. You could roughen or tear the edges a little bit, too. Make the places where you think fingers would touch the page to turn it over a little darker.

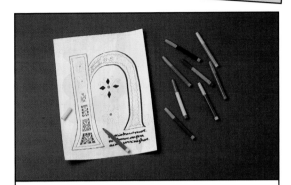

▲ **3.** Color your design using felt-tip pens. To complete it, highlight some parts with the gold felt-tip pen.

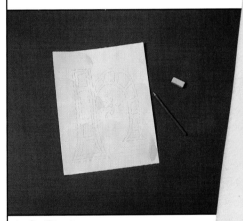

▲ **2.** Design your page carefully in pencil. Make one big letter with decorations or little pictures to take up most of the page, then add some smaller writing at the end. You could copy the manuscripts on pages 13 or 20 or make up your own design using your name.

21

THE RULERS OF BRITAIN

When the Anglo-Saxons first came to Britain, they lived in small family groups. As they took control of more of England, they became organized into larger groups with a local chief or king. The names given to the areas under each king remain today in some British county names. If Essex means "the kingdom of the East Saxons," what do you think Wessex and Sussex might mean?

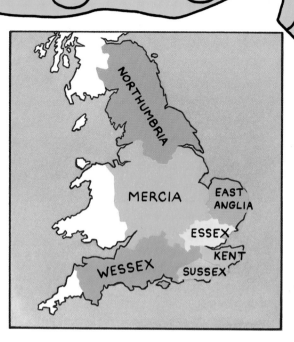

As well as the main kingdoms shown on the map, there were probably many independent kings ruling small areas.

Each person had a different place and a different value in the kingdom. The Anglo-Saxons actually developed a system called "wergild" to set a value on people. This meant that each person was worth an amount of money.

The king was worth a lot of money, while a slave was worth very little. Everyone else came somewhere in between. If a person was killed, the killer had to pay the victim's family the amount he or she was worth.

As some of the kingdoms became more powerful, they tried to take over neighboring areas. The first man to call himself "King of the English" was Offa, king of Mercia. His power and influence reached into the other kingdoms south of the River Humber.

▲*This great bank of earth with a ditch running beside it was built on the orders of King Offa. It is 148 miles (238 km) long, stretching the length of Wales and separating it from Mercia. We don't know for certain why Offa's Dyke was built, but it shows that he was very powerful.*

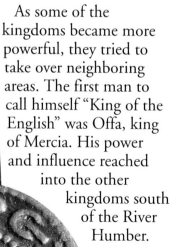

◀ *Offa had coins made with his name stamped on them.*

22

Offa ruled from 757 to 796, but by the time of his death, a new danger was threatening the peace of Britain. Once again, raiders from northern Europe were attacking. In 793, Vikings attacked and destroyed the monastery at Lindisfarne.

The Vikings were excellent seamen and fierce fighters who came from Denmark, Norway, and Sweden. For over 200 years they raided the coasts of Europe, but as traders they traveled even farther – to Russia and central Asia. Some people think that they reached America as well, 600 years before Christopher Columbus.

Many of the Vikings who attacked Britain came from Denmark and were known as Danes, Northmen, or Norsemen.

The Anglo-Saxons were very afraid of the Viking raiders. A common prayer was, "From the fury of the Northmen, good Lord deliver us."

ALFRED AND LATER KINGS

At first the Vikings were mainly interested in raiding – taking what valuables they could find and disappearing again. But as time went on, the Vikings wanted more from Britain. Like the Anglo-Saxons before them, they did not have enough farming land at home to feed everyone and needed to find new lands. In 860, a large army of Vikings arrived from Denmark. The Anglo-Saxons called these Danes the "Great Army."

The Great Army attacked East Anglia and Northumbria and killed their kings. Then they moved into Mercia. Finally, only Wessex was not controlled by the new invaders.

ALFRED "THE GREAT"

When a man called Alfred became King of Wessex, the Danes had already been attacking for some time. The leader of the Great Army, Guthrun, attacked Alfred at Chippenham during the Christmas celebrations, forcing the king to escape and hide at Athelney, in the marshes of Somerset. But from there, Alfred organized his forces and defeated the Danes at Edington in 878.

▲*After their defeat in 878, the Danes agreed to settle in the area shown in orange.*

DANELAW

The Danes agreed to leave Wessex, part of Mercia, and southeast England alone and to settle in Northumbria, East Anglia, and the rest of Mercia. This area was known as Danelaw. Guthrun became a Christian.

◀ *After defeating the Danes, Alfred built fortified towns, called "burhs," where people could be safe if the Danes attacked again. This is where our word "borough" comes from. Like Roman towns hundreds of years before, Alfred's burhs had a rectangular shape and straight streets. This is a photograph of Wareham, Dorset, where the burh's street plan can still be seen.*

This jewel was found in 1693, near Athelney. Words around the jewel say, "Aelfred mec heht gewyrcan" meaning "Alfred had me made." It shows what a wealthy and powerful man Alfred was.

THE IMPORTANCE OF LEARNING

Although he himself only learned to read and write when he was grown up, Alfred was concerned about the Anglo-Saxon language and education.

He had several important Latin books translated into Anglo-Saxon, which is an early form of the modern English language. The Anglo-Saxon Chronicle was begun by him. Alfred's actions helped to create the feeling of a country with a history – an idea of "Englishness."

While Alfred made his position safe in the south, more and more Vikings settled in northern England, trading with other parts of Europe. Wealthy towns grew up at places such as York and Nottingham.

ENGLAND AFTER ALFRED

It was Alfred's grandson, Athelstan, who, 50 years after Alfred fled to Athelney, marched his armies north and made the Viking and Welsh kings swear loyalty to him. For the first time, one man really was King of England, with most of Wales and Scotland also under his rule. But Athelstan and the kings who came after him still had battles to fight.

THE LAST CONQUEROR

Nearly 40 years after Athelstan's death, the Vikings once again began to attack Britain. King Ethelred agreed to pay money to the Danes if they would go home! This was called "Danegeld," and for a while it worked. But in 1013, King Swein of Denmark attacked and seized the throne, beginning nearly 30 years of Danish rule.

Saxons
924 – 39 Athelstan
939 – 46 Edmund
946 – 55 Edred
955 – 59 Edwy
959 – 75 Edgar
975 – 78 Edward (the Martyr)
978 – 1013 Ethelred (the Unready)

Danes
1013 – 14 Swein
1014 – 35 Cnut
1035 – 40 Harold I
1040 – 42 Harthacnut

Saxons
1042 – 66 Edward the Confessor
1066 Harold II

Normans
William I (the Conqueror)

Swein's son, Cnut, married Emma, the widow of Ethelred. She was a Norman princess from Normandy in northern France. When Edward the Confessor died without any children in 1066, he promised the throne to William, the Duke of Normandy, but the English decided to crown Harold, the Earl of Wessex instead.

As soon as Harold was crowned, he faced trouble. The Norwegians invaded northern England in September and Harold marched north to defeat them. In the meantime, William landed in Sussex to claim the throne. Harold's exhausted army met the Normans at Hastings and Harold was killed.

The Bayeux tapestry, which shows the story of William's claim to the English throne, was embroidered by Anglo-Saxon women in France. This part shows the death of King Harold.

William's coronation on Christmas Day, 1066, marked the end of Anglo-Saxon rule in England, but William's position was not yet secure. Accepting the crown of the Anglo-Saxon kings was one of his first acts to take control of the kingdom.

◀ *This engraving shows William being crowned King of England at Westminster Abbey.*

MAKE WILLIAM'S CROWN

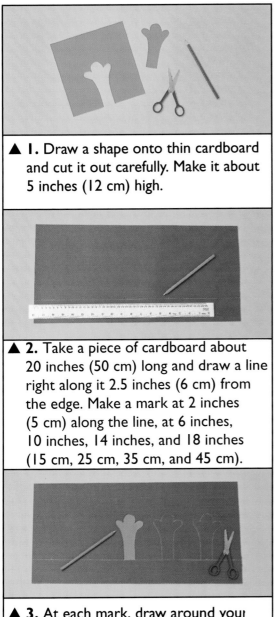

▲ **1.** Draw a shape onto thin cardboard and cut it out carefully. Make it about 5 inches (12 cm) high.

▲ **2.** Take a piece of cardboard about 20 inches (50 cm) long and draw a line right along it 2.5 inches (6 cm) from the edge. Make a mark at 2 inches (5 cm) along the line, at 6 inches, 10 inches, 14 inches, and 18 inches (15 cm, 25 cm, 35 cm, and 45 cm).

▲ **3.** At each mark, draw around your cardboard shape above the line to form the crown.

> **You will need:** thin cardboard or posterboard • a ruler • a pencil • scissors • gold paint • paper clips or tape

4. Carefully cut out the crown and paint it gold. Fix the two ends together with paper clips or tape, overlapping the ends to give a good fit.

THE INVADERS LEGACY

All the invaders of Britain from the Romans to the Normans have left traces of their lives that can still be seen today.

PLACE NAMES
The names of British towns and villages are clues to who lived there in the past. The Romans, the Anglo-Saxons, and the Vikings used their own languages to name places. Sometimes the spelling of these has changed over the years. Look at the lists below. Then find a map of England, choose any area, and see if you can tell which people named the towns and villages nearby. Books about place-names in your local library will give you even more information about their meaning.

Roman place-names

camp	=	plain
caster	=	fort
eccles	=	church
port	=	harbor
wic	=	town

Anglo-Saxon place-names

burg, borough	=	fortified place
den, dene	=	valley
ea, ey	=	river
feld, field	=	field
ford	=	shallow river crossing
ham	=	settlement home
head	=	hill
holt	=	dense wood
ing	=	people
lea, leigh, ley	=	clearing
mere	=	lake
sted, stead	=	place
stoke, stow	=	meeting place
ton, tun	=	farm or village
wald	=	wood
wic, wick, wich	=	farm
worth	=	hedged land

Viking place-names

by	=	village
thorpe	=	small village

THE ENGLISH LANGUAGE
Some of our names for the days of the week also come from Britain's invaders. Sunday and Monday are named after the sun and moon, while Saturday takes its name from the Roman god, Saturn. Look at pages 18 and 19 and see if you can work out where the names of the other days of the week come from.

Many other common English words come from Anglo-Saxon. Below are a few of them:

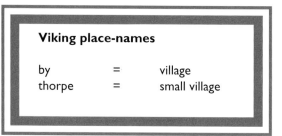

cald, penig, cyssan, grund, abbod, lang, Englisc, gewyrcan

Can you guess what they mean? Look at the box on the left if you get stuck.

Answers The Anglo-Saxon words mean: cold, penny, kiss, ground, abbot, long, English. Look on page 24 for a clue to "gewyrcan" and remember that in order to make something, you have to "work."

28

DID YOU KNOW?

Until about 9,000 years ago, Britain was joined to the rest of Europe. People could simply walk across. But gradually the sea rose and Britain became an island. The only way to reach it was by boat.

When the Emperor Claudius came to Colchester to accept the surrender of some British leaders, he even brought a few elephants along to impress the Britons with his power! Of course, they had never seen such creatures before.

One way of writing Anglo-Saxon words was to use "runes." You can see which letters the runes stood for below. The Anglo-Saxons seem to have thought that the runes themselves were magic. They wrote the alphabet on rings as a charm against illness and danger.

In a way, the Vikings really did succeed in conquering Britain. The Normans who invaded in 1066 were descended from "Norsemen" who had settled in northern France 200 years earlier.

The legend of King Arthur and his knights of the round table is set in the period when Anglo-Saxon raiders were attacking British tribes. All the old writings about Arthur date from hundreds of years later, so it is very hard to tell whether a British king called Arthur really existed.

ᚠ ᚢ ᚦ ᚩ ᚱ ᚳ ᚷ ᚹ ᚻ ᚾ ᛁ ᛉ ᛄ ᛈ
f u t o r k g w h n i j h p

ᛏ ᛋ ᛏ ᛒ ᛖ ᛗ ᛚ ᛝ ᛞ ᛟ ᚪ ᚫ ᚣ ᛠ
x s t b e m l ng d oe a ae y ea

29

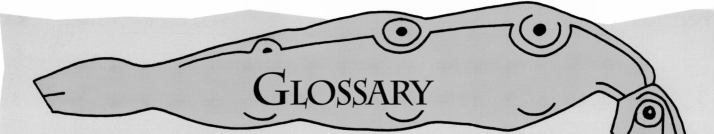

GLOSSARY

archaeologist – someone who studies objects from past times, often those that are buried in the ground.

burh – a fortified town that King Alfred ordered to be built.

Danegeld – money paid by Anglo-Saxon kings to Danish leaders to try to stop them from invading Britain.

daub – mud or clay used to fill the gaps in walls made of wattle.

earthwork – a structure made mainly of earth and stones, often as a place of safety.

empire – a large area of land, often made up of different countries, ruled over by one person, an emperor or empress.

forum – the main square and market place of a Roman town.

inscription – written words, especially those on a building, gravestone or coin.

invader – a person who moves into a new area without the permission of people already living there.

javelin – a kind of spear that could be thrown at the enemy.

legion – a body of between 3,000 and 6,000 men in the Roman army.

missionary – a person who tries to convert others to a particular religious faith.

monastery – a place where monks live – Christians who live together to devote their lives to God.

monument – a building or statue put up to remind people of a person or event.

rudder – a piece of wood under a boat that can be turned to change the boat's direction.

settler – a person who makes his or her home in a new place.

torque – a necklace of twisted metal made by the ancient Britons.

vellum – calf's skin made smooth so that it could be written on.

wattle – twigs woven together to make walls.

wergild – an Anglo-Saxon system of setting a value of money on each person. If the person was killed, the killer could pay that money to the family of the victim and avoid further punishment.

RESOURCES

BOOKS TO READ

There are many books on this period of British history. You should find some in your local or school library. A few to look out for are:

Birkett, Alaric. *Vikings,* Chester Springs, Penn.: Dufour, 1985.

Briais, Bernard. *Celts,* Bellmore, N.Y.: Marshall Cavendish, 1991.

Burrell, Roy. *The Romans,* New York: Oxford University Press, 1991.

Clare, J., ed. *Vikings,* San Diego: Harcourt Brace, 1992.

Dineen, Jacqueline. *The Romans,* New York: Macmillan, 1992.

Martell, Hazel. *The Vikings,* New York: Macmillan, 1992.

What Do We Know About the Celts?, New York: Simon and Schuster, 1993.

Odijk, Pamela. *The Ancient Britons,* New York: Macmillan, 1989.

The Romans, Morristown, N.J.: Silver Burdett Press, 1989.

The Vikings, Morristown, N.J.: Silver Burdett Press, 1990.

Wright, Rachel. *Vikings,* New York: Franklin Watts, 1992.